Easy Concertos
and Concertinos
for Violin and Piano

T0056408

F. Küchler

Concertino
in D

Op. 12
(1st and 3rd position)

Bosworth

CONCERTINO

⟨I.–III. Position⟩

I

Ferdinand Küchler, op. 12

Copyright MCMXXXVI by Bosworth & Co.

B. & Co. 19044
Made in England

Tous droits d'exécution réservés

poco a poco ritardando

II.

Andante cantabile

CONCERTINO

⟨I.–III. Position⟩

g.B. = mit dem ganzen Bogen. – Whole Bow. – Tout l'archet.

u.H. = mit der unteren Hälfte des Bogens. – Lower Half of the Bow. – Moitié inférieure de l'archet.

o.H. = mit der oberen Hälfte des Bogens. – Upper Half of the Bow. – Moitié supérieure de l'archet.

M. = mit der Mitte. – In the Middle. – Au milieu.

Sp. = an der Spitze. – At the Tip. – À la pointe.

Fr. = am Frosch. – At the nut. – Au talon.

simile = ähnlich, ebenso, d.h. das Folgende so spielen wie das Vorhergehende.
= "like" i.e. play the following in the same way as the preceding.
= semblable c. à. d. interpréter cette partie de la même manière que la précédente.

· · · · · = feste kurze Striche. – Detached. – Détaché court.

– – – – = breite (geschobene) Striche. – Broad bowing. – Largement détaché.

❘ ❘ ❘ ❘ = geworfene Striche (und Springbogen). – Spiccato (and springing). – Jeté (et sautillé).

⨪ ⨪ ⨪ ⨪ = fest gestoßene Striche mit viel Bogen. – Detached but much bow. – Coups détachés ferme avec beau-
[coup d'archet.

Violino   **I**   Ferdinand Küchler, op. 12

Copyright MCMXXXVI by Bosworth & Co.   B. & Co. 19044   *Tous droits d'exécution réservés*

II.

Flageolet ad lib.

RONDO
III
Allegretto

un poco rit. *ten.* a tempo

*) Performance:
*) Ausführung:
*) Exécution:

B. & Co. 19044

4

*) The square note ⟨♦⟩ is to be stopped ⟨as auxiliary note in shifting⟩ but is not to be played.

*) Eine eckige Note ⟨♦⟩ wird nur gegriffen ⟨als Hilfsnote für den Lagenwechsel⟩, aber nicht gespielt.

*) Une note accessoire ⟨♦⟩ ne doit être qu'appuyée ⟨comme note intermédiaire pour le changement de position⟩ mais non exécutée.

B.& Co.19044

III.

RONDO
Allegretto

un poco rit.   ten.   a tempo

un poco rallentando   a tempo

tranquillo   ritardando